Plate I

DEDHAM MILL

(London. Victoria and Albert Museum, No. 34)

JOHN CONSTABLE, R.A.

JOHN CONSTABLE, R.A.

By

The Hon. ANDREW SHIRLEY

LONDON

THE MEDICI SOCIETY, LTD.

By the same Author

The Published Mezzotints
of David Lucas, after
John Constable, R.A.

Bonington

Memoirs of the Life of John Constable
by C. R. Leslie
(Edited and Enlarged)

PRINTED IN GREAT BRITAIN BY HENRY STONE AND SON LTD., BANBURY

FIRST PUBLISHED MCMXLIV   REPRINTED MCMXLVIII

JOHN CONSTABLE, R.A.

A PICTURE can take our attention for one or other of many reasons. The best of all is the quality of the painting itself, and ultimately that is the only good reason for looking at any series of pictures. But there are other appeals ; for instance, Watteau's capacity to idealize one facet of his age gives an aroma to his creations to-day that they had not in his lifetime. The impact of a Michael Angelo, whose style reverberates through the schools of painting down to the eighteenth century, is a fact in the history of taste. The technical innovations of Van Eyck have their own interest ; so, too, does a temperament such as Blake's, which left him in so many ways isolated from his generation.

These interests have nothing to do with æsthetic quality, and can be found in second-rate artists. In so far as they are human and historical, they add a flavour to appreciation, and in looking at Constable's pictures, it does no harm to reflect that round him, an Englishman, centred the revival of landscape in the nineteenth century, and that, though his method is familiar and almost old-masterish to-day, his contemporaries regarded him as revolutionary and, some would have added, shocking.

To get the spice of Constable's work it is really important to appreciate this fact. It is a sad thing that most people who think for themselves or see for themselves are considered odd by their contemporaries. "When I am painting, I try to forget that I have ever seen a picture," he wrote. This was heresy from a man born in an age of established eclecticism : but a splendid principle for any painter. "However one's mind may be elevated and kept up to what is excellent by the works of the Great Masters," he writes elsewhere, "still Nature is the fountain's head, the source from which all originality must spring."

As Constable grew up, everything in landscape was Claude, Poussin, or Salvator Rosa, variously degraded by second-rate impersonators. It is true that in literature Romanticism had already made an advance, and the Picturesque, which was accepted in garden design, and in watercolour, had begun to influence the painters' choice of subject. But the æsthetic of Reynolds' *Discourses* still held sway, and "ideal form" had ousted observation from the painters' curriculum. It is remarkable how quickly Constable saw his objective in art—"a pure and unaffected representation of the scenes that may employ me." "There is room enough for a natural painter . . . the great vice of the day is Bravura," he concluded in 1802, the year he first exhibited at the Academy. A year before he had criticized someone's landscape in words which revealed his own outlook—"There is plenty of light without any light at all." He knew by this time what he wanted to do and what he did not want to be.

Later he elaborated, as was natural, his thesis, and of all people, that dismal painter of vast canvases, West, helped him with a phrase—"Light and shade never stand still." Constable developed a theory which he called the Chiaroscuro of Nature, by which he meant that " there are no lines in nature ". Everything is seen by the eye in terms of dark and light masses. This doctrine, in fact, became the core of nineteenth-century painting from the Barbizon School to the Pointillistes, and one sees its results in Constable's latest pictures, such as *Arundel Mill and Castle* (Plate 150), painted mainly with the palette knife.

There was something logical in his search for technique. Not that Constable had a cold-hearted personality—he moved rapidly from laughter to anger ; warm in affection, generous in praise, vinegar as a critic. He could exclaim like any romantic " Paint me a desolation ", but he reverted constantly to such phrases as " I am determined that my pictures should have chiaroscuro if they have nothing else,"—a composition balanced in terms of light and colour. " Do you not find it very difficult to determine where to place your brown tree ? " said his friend, Sir George Beaumont, the patron and amateur painter. " Not in the least," said Constable, " I never use such a thing." This formula of classical composition, stereotyped from Claude's invention, had no place in his idiom.

Essentially he was more of a realist than a romantic. His love of order, which he called his lack of imagination, and his admiration for Claude and Cozens saved him even in his most impassioned and dramatic moments from the tendency of English Romantics to neglect form. Colour became to him an adjunct, not the prime consideration, as soon as he had succeeded in his first main experiment in painting—the attempt to match the natural tints in landscape, to escape from the brown tree to the green tree, and to key the whole colour scheme to the higher scale of sunlight. He was not the only Englishman then making this effort ; for Cotman, Turner, Bonington and the Fieldings, all were on the same path, to name only a few. But peculiar to his nature was the country bias—"All health and the absence of anything stagnant," or " The sound of water escaping from milldams, willows, old rotten planks, slimy posts and brickwork—I love such things ". No other painter smelt the land or felt it through his boots in this way.

An analysis of his pictures shows clearly how their essential appeal and their satisfying quality depends on the balance of tones, not of colours, Black and white reproductions of canvases pre-eminent at first sight for their colour values bring out this characteristic. The *Salisbury Cathedral from the Meadows* (Plate 120*a*), or the *Hampstead Heath* (Plate 84), or the *Study of Tree Stems* (Plate 116)—examples could be multiplied indefinitely to show Constable's quality as a designer in mass, the quality by which Cézanne is in a measure related to him.

This appreciation of design by the artist and the spectator is the intellectual rather than the emotional side of art. With all his capacity for emotion—he was " thrown into a perspiration " by discussing religion with an Irvingite—Constable's intelligence was well developed and survived the ineptitude of a flogging usher at Lavenham Grammar School to react happily to the stimulus of his friend Archdeacon Fisher's greater knowledge. One finds him, for instance, reading Sharon Turner's *History of the Anglo-Saxons*, though novels were beyond him ; he never read for distraction. More indicative of his bent is such a phrase as : " The sister arts have less hold on my mind . . . than the sciences, especially the science of geology which, more than any other, seems to satisfy my mind."

The scientist in Constable is the realist who, as a painter, inquires elaborately into cloud formations ; what they portend, and what produces them, so that, by complete knowledge, he can the better delineate them. And indeed, a distinguished meteorologist, Mr. L. Bonacina, has shown that imitations of his work can often be detected because a cloud form has been introduced which, atmospherically, is impossible in the structure of the sky. Constable was meticulous in observing the moods of the day, and a number of studies of cloud forms exist (e.g. Plates 96–98) which carry additional notes on the direction and force of the wind, as well as the hour, day, and month of the sketch.

The sky, moreover, was vital to his conception of landscape. It typifies movement ; it is never constant, and so to seize one moment is to give the character of the scene. His was an instantaneous art. What Northcote said, comparing Reynolds with the Old Masters, is truer still of Constable : " They painted hours ; he painted moments." " The sky is the source of light in Nature, and governs everything," writes Constable ; but he goes on : " The difficulty of skies in painting is very great . . . because with all their brilliancy, they ought not to come forward, or, indeed, to be thought of any more than extreme distances are ; but this does not apply to the phenomena or accidental effects of the sky, because they always particularly attract." This was a major problem for any painter, both in composition and execution, and one that at last Constable solved happily ; but a problem essential in its importance to a man who believed that there is no " class of landscape in which the sky is not the keynote, the standard of scale, the chief organ of sentiment ". Not for nothing was Constable, like Rembrandt, a miller's son, whose livelihood depended on the wind. If the sky was misjudged and the sails set wrong, there was too little power or too much, and loss in either case. Before he had become a painter, Constable's eye had been trained to judge the anatomy of the sky, just as Rabelais, Smollett, and sundry doctors of lower literary standing had been educated as scientific observers before they found they had a gift for writing.

This faculty of observing and interpreting the values of natural light in a higher scale of colour than had been attempted before made his contribution to European art. In 1822, a Paris dealer, John Arrowsmith, first made contact with Constable and tried to buy *The Haywain* for exhibition in Paris. Negotiations were protracted, but in 1824 it was hung in the Salon, together with a *Hampstead Heath* and *A View on the Stour*. This exhibition made history, and it can be argued that Delacroix, and, through him, the Barbizon school, and through them the main valuable current of modern French painting, derived their force from the English pictures shown there, and from Constable in particular. His approach to painting was not new to the French in every sense. Bonington and Thales and Newton Fielding had already been working in Paris for a few years, and as early as 1820 Géricault had written to Delacroix that he must come to London to study the English School. What Constable had to give was not only the new colour scale and the movement of light, but a new technique that interpreted these fresh ideas with an intellectual assurance to which everything in Delacroix's mentality responded, a technique, moreover, that by luck derived from Rubens, who at that moment was the god of the younger French painters in Paris. And how the pundits and the critics argued ! The older school began by saying that no true view could be formed of Constable's painting until he had essayed " les sites majestueux et enchanteurs de l'Italie ", but Delécluze, their Sampson, ended on a defeatist note : " Malgré tous nos discours la nouvelle école l'emportera. La chose est peutêtre déjà faite."

Official recognition at last came down on Constable's side, and he was awarded the Gold Medal, and received a similar honour from the city of Lille where *The White Horse* was exhibited in the following year. It must also have been the Salon exhibition which led Delacroix to follow Géricault's advice, for in 1825 he made the journey to England with Bonington and young Isabey and actually called on Constable with a letter of introduction, though unluckily the two missed each other. However, opportunities of studying Constable's work in Paris were not confined to this single exhibition, nor to the Salon of 1827, in which a " Paysage avec Figures et Animaux " hung between a Corot and a Bonington. Arrowsmith was an active purchaser, and had a Constable room in his gallery ; and a more powerful dealer, Louis Schroth, also purchased several of Constable's works. Counting private orders, not less than twenty-four canvases were sent over to France between 1824 and 1826, when, unfortunately, an economic blizzard destroyed Arrowsmith's finances and crippled Schroth. We hear no more of Arrowsmith, and Schroth retired upon his old business as a print-seller, which locked up less of his capital than oil-paintings.

This, then, is Constable's claim upon history as a creative and directive influence upon the course of painting, apart from the intrinsic merit of his pictures. The years 1824–6 were the climax of his career and popularity ; he was full of commissions and actually employing an assistant. Had he not been so irremediably English, he might have accepted the pressing invitations to cross the Channel, and perhaps the stronger impression of his personality would have made easier the path of the younger French painters who were to become the Men of 1830, and who were to be denied the official approval of the Salon for nearly twenty years. Even so, there must have been some legend about Constable's personality and conversation current in Paris, for in a letter of 1844 Delacroix quotes some remarks of Constable's on the different greens in nature, of which I know no other printed source, and in 1848 wrote to Silvestre the famous panegyric in which he calls Constable " la gloire de l'école anglaise ". This Continental fame had only a slight repercussion on Constable's standing in England. Wilkie, who of the Academicians was at least his friend, was astonished to see how fine his work looked in the Paris setting ; he had been unable to recognize its quality fully at home. Yet, in 1824, at the age of forty-eight, he was still only an A.R.A., and did not attain full rank until 1829. His whole progress whether technically or in public favour had always been extremely slow, and he did not have a picture accepted at the Academy until 1802, the year in which Turner, his senior by one year, was elected R.A.

From the start he had faced opposition. His father, a prosperous miller, saw, as many other fathers have done, a menace rather than a profit to the family fortunes in an artistic career for his son. For two years, indeed, after his first efforts in oil, assisted by the local housepainter, John Dunthorne, and after an unfruitful journey to London, he was ordered to give up his art and stick to milling. As one looks through the early drawings and the first oils one is hardly surprised at the decision ; it must have been difficult to see, through the clumsiness of the handling, that they contained the germs of a positive vision and intelligence. At times, one may quarrel with Constable's statement in 1802 that he had no trouble with drawing. What I fancy he meant by this was that his grasp of perspective was complete ; and indeed the strong distinction of the planes in composition is characteristic of his work from the start. It is, in fact, an intellectual quality planted in him that expressed itself in the search for the Chiaroscuro of Nature.

His first ten years of serious work from 1801 to 1811 form a period of experiment, as is natural. He had to find a means of getting a clearer and more delicate representation of natural colour than Ruysdael, his favourite among Dutch painters, had achieved. He had to study Wilson's sunlight, Girtin's breadth, and everything about Gainsborough. Gainsborough, perhaps, was the most important master for him ; his influence is most strongly marked between 1800 and 1805, for his roots ran back through Van Dyck to Rubens, and to Flemish colour schemes more brilliant and dashing than the Dutch had used. There are, indeed, two landscapes, *A Hilly Landscape* (Plate 154) and the *Landscape Composition* (Plate 153), which give the first oblique hint of Constable's preoccupation with Rubens. The first is now well-known as a picture, but the second gathers up English watercolour as Cozens and Girtin left it, embroidering it with open touches that are Constable's own, and embodying it into almost the most majestic composition that he ever achieved. It is a studio piece crossbred from his tour to the Lakes in 1806 and the study of the late sixteenth-century masters of the Low Countries.

By 1811 he had advanced to a completely personal style ; fresh, delicate, and intimate in its view of the countryside. The clearest example of it was his Academy picture of that year, *Dedham Vale* (Plate 40), among the first to achieve favourable notice, or indeed any notice at all from the contemporary critics. This, of course, was a finished canvas, and on a fair scale—one finds him experimenting far ahead of this technique in his smaller sketches, and *Locks and Cottages on the Stour* (Plate 41), painted probably in the same year, shows far greater movement and vivacity than the Academy set piece. It is, indeed, an instantaneous sketch splashed on between showers.

The story of Constable's private life is either small beer or near tragedy ; the verdict depends on the amount of attention paid to its detail. It is, in fact, a very ordinary story, the highlights and shadows being those common to everyday men, but as a great artist he had the power to interpret his experience, and the moods of his life colour his approach to landscape. It was about 1811 that he fell in love with a girl he had known for many years as a visitor to East Bergholt. Maria Bicknell was the grand-daughter of the Rector, Doctor Rhudde, a rich and angry man. Her parents, also, were unfortunately well-to-do, her father being solicitor to the Admiralty. Though she had accepted Constable by 1811, for five years her parents feared to offend old Doctor Rhudde, from whom they had great expectations, by sanctioning the match. Meanwhile, John's financial position was too slender before his father's death in 1816 to withstand the responsibility of marrying a delicate wife.

The correspondence that passed between John and Maria during those years, despite, or because of, extreme simplicity of language, makes a vivid and touching picture of their characters. John's was a mercurial temperament, shifting from optimism to depression, stung by neglect as an artist and as a suitor, yet sustained by an inner core of self-reliance and tenacity : her nature on the other hand is quieter, at the outset almost in danger of being colourless, but through her gentle affection now and again one perceives the flash of stubbornness on matters of principle, the brave ability to criticize her lover despite her pride in him—qualities of honesty which were essential for so honest a painter to find in his wife. And when once Maria had decided that she had paid, in five years, her full duty to her father and mother, she walked out on them.

She and John were married at St. Martin's in the Fields by his friend John Fisher, the Archdeacon of Berkshire, a classic friend. They married on about £350 a year, and there is a note that about this time the Inland

Revenue officials of the day did not recognize his earnings from his profession as constituting an income. However, he set out to humour the world without deviating from his artistic principles, and during the early years of a marriage to which seven children were born he spent more time on portraiture than has in the past been recognized.

The cycle of portraits reproduced here shows his progress from incapacity to competence and, in one of two instances, to brilliant achievement. The portrait of *Mrs. Constable Asleep* (Plate 110) and the *Portrait of a Girl* (Plate 160, conceivably his daughter, Maria) are technically and emotionally of a very high order. So, too, his *Mrs. Pulham of Woodbridge*, the wife of an old Suffolk friend and patron that now hangs, a flashing piece of colour, in the Metropolitan Museum in New York. At the time of his marriage, however, his portraits though competent and attractive—for instance, *William Watts Russell* (Plate 13) or *Dr. Wingfield* (Plate 13*a*)—belong to the Reynolds–Hoppner tradition, in which he was immersed when he was employed to copy portraits at Ham House in 1807. This time was not wasted, even from the point of view of his landscape. It is a commonplace that Reynolds' portraits translate with beautiful ease into mezzotint ; they depend pre-eminently upon chiaroscuro, the balance of tone. In studying Reynolds' flesh painting and his skilful control over its tone value, Constable was also learning to control his skies, so that " with all their brilliancy, they should not come forward ".

In the happiness of his marriage, which his in-laws gradually came to accept, Constable's art opens into full flower. In 1815 he had shown at the Academy a carefully finished work, *Boatbuilding, Flatford* (Plate 53) which, in those days, was a portent, because it had been painted entirely in the open air. Even so, it does not quite catch the brilliancy of colour which one finds in the National Gallery *Weymouth Bay* (Plate 58), conceived on his honeymoon, or sketches of the valleys round Salisbury at the Victoria and Albert Museum or in Mr. T. W. Bacon's collection (Plate 72*a*).

1821 was a rich year of painting with the *Cathedral Close, Salisbury* (Plate 64), and the silvery *Distant View of Salisbury* (Plate 62), which recalls Constable's description of his journey to the Beckford Sale at Fonthill, how the spire " darted up into the sky like a needle ". It was in the early '20s that he made an essential technical discovery which enabled him to progress beyond the beautiful and luminous style he had built up. Earlier paintings, such as the *Landscape Composition* (Plate 153) and the *Autumnal Sunset* (Plate 44), show that he was not unaware of Rubens as a painter ; yet for all his panegyrics on Claude and Ruysdael, he hardly mentions Rubens in his correspondence. But once he had learnt from him to exchange the grey foundation of the traditional English School for a warmer brown, he found a key that would hold his most brilliant tones together and permit him to make further technical innovations. An unfinished picture, *Greenwich Palace* (Plate 157), dating about 1821, is positive evidence of the new method. *Salisbury Cathedral from the Bishop's Garden* (Plate VI) is perhaps the first picture of substantial size painted in the new technique, which also is shown in the monochrome sketch for it in Mr. T. W. Bacon's collection (Plate 81). It is significant, too, that in the same autumn, he stayed with Sir George Beaumont at Cole Orton, arguing still, no doubt, as to process, discussing, as we know, contemporary literature, but, above all, copying most carefully the brilliant *Château de Steen*, which Sir George bequeathed to the National Gallery (Plate 8*a*).

The mood of his painting continues happy and calm—*Stratford Mill*, 1820 (Pl. 61), *The Haywain*, 1821 (Pl. V), *The Leaping Horse*, 1825 (Pl. IX), and *The Cornfield*, 1826 (Pl. X). He was supported by the patronage of Archdeacon Fisher and by the flush of success and reputation that came from the exhibition of his works in Paris. Perhaps *The Cornfield* and *The Glebe Farm* (Plate 102) are the culmination of the big Academy compositions of this period, compositions that were carefully built up in the studio from sketches and preliminary studies, as may be seen from the illustrations. One must mention, too, *The Devil's Dyke, near Brighton* (Plate 159), painted about 1826 ; a canvas of surpassing boldness of which the simplicity in structure at first sight is deceptive. No one, however, could fail to recognize the gleaming handling of the sky which anticipates the famous glittering lights that Constable gave to the *Hadleigh Castle* (Plate 111), the *Hampstead Heath* (Plate XII) and other later works. It was a scene that particularly arrested him, and he and Mrs. Constable both recurred to it in the correspondence. And yet Constable felt himself, in painting it, to be attempting almost the impossible ; " it is the business of a painter," he wrote about that time, " not to contend with nature, and put a valley filled with imagery fifty miles long on a canvas of a few inches, but to attempt to make something out of nothing, in attempting which he must almost of necessity become poetical." " My art," he said another time in contrast, " can be found under every hedge."

As anyone who looks through the reproductions in this book must quickly see, Constable found his subjects in quite a few neighbourhoods. He did not need variety of scene to stimulate him : a shift of the clouds would produce a new pattern of colours and shadows over Hampstead Heath or the Vale of Dedham. The very sameness or familiarity of the views, so differently handled in terms of light and shade, gives almost an abstract quality to an art which has been criticized as concentrating over-much on exact reproduction. But, above all, he never painted his best without some form of personal affection for the countryside in which he was working. The Stour Valley, Hampstead, Wiltshire, and Dorsetshire, Brighton, and Sussex, the fields of his main activities, were all endeared to him by special ties. At East Bergholt he was born, and the green mile across the valley to Dedham is the scene of endless sketches ; the valley, he himself said, made him a painter ; and it only drops out as a principal source of inspiration when his marriage had embroiled him with Dr. Rhudde and made visits with his wife an acid social problem. Luckily his friendship with Fisher had already introduced him to the country round Salisbury. Subjects from Wiltshire and Dorset, where he spent his honeymoon near the surprisingly red cliffs of Osmington Mills, predominate from 1816 to 1824, recurring frequently until Fisher's sudden death in 1832. In the mid-'twenties, for the sake of his family's health, he moved from Charlotte Street to the Hampstead hills, where skies and heath scenery were ready at hand for him. In fact, in his attachment to places he was very like the old Essex labourer, of whom he used to tell the story that on moving to another village five miles away he paused on the crest of a hill to look back at his old home, exclaiming : " Farewell, old England ; perhaps I may never see you more." In the 'twenties, he went often to Brighton for Mrs. Constable's sake, who was already ailing ; but though the downs were enjoyable and the foreshores gave him many new subjects in the vein that Collins had done much to popularize, he never cared for the place, considering the beach scenes only fit for a display of technique, without any charge of emotion.

After Mrs. Constable's death he seldom stayed there, and never for any length of time, only going down when a child's health made it necessary. Brighton, he felt, was a travesty of the country ; and his general attitude is best shown by a phrase late in life, that he " wished to promote the study of the Rural Scenery of England, with all its endearing associations, its amenities, and even in its most simple localities." This explains readily enough why he did not repeat his visits to Derbyshire and the Lakes, and why he found so much pleasure in his last discovery, Sussex, introduced to him by a new friend and namesake, George Constable. It reminded him of Suffolk in many ways—" woods, lanes, single trees, rivers, cottages, barns, mills, and above all such beautiful heath scenery."

Mrs. Constable, " My Darling Fish " as he called her, died in November, 1828, of consumption ; and his twelve years of happiness were over. For all its brilliant sparkle, *The Chain Pier, Brighton*, of 1827 (Plate 106), is overcast with the threat of storm. " Every gleam of sunshine is blighted to me," he exclaimed ; " can it be wondered at that I paint continual storms." Fisher and Charles Leslie rallied to his support ; but the evaporation of happiness and of his moment of success combined with ill-health and fits of depression to magnify irritations into disasters. During his last period from 1828 to his death in 1837 his art may be said to lose something in warmth, but to gain in drama and in power and variety of execution.

His election to the Academy in 1829, long delayed by faction, came almost as an insult a few months after his wife's death. " I am solitary and cannot impart it," he quoted from Dr. Johnson. He had never enjoyed much success with the public, though he had a small coterie of friends and patrons. The Paris medal had brought no further increase of reputation in England. He had not Turner's gift as a salesman. Turner refused to sell a given picture, because secretly he wished to leave it to the nation, but he could use the refusal to screw Gillott up to another purchase. Constable, however, would refuse a picture, because he wasn't going to sell it, because inwardly he felt it was " too important in his practice " to be parted with —and that was that. Actually he sold fairly steadily in a small way for the last twenty years of his life ; but he did not get high prices, nor did his scale advance much. For instance, *The White Horse* and the *Stratford Mill* were sold in 1820 for £100 each ; *The Glebe Farm* went to Sheepshanks for £150 in 1827, and in 1835 he had £250 from Vernon for *The Valley Farm*—half what Turner or Collins would have charged for a canvas of the same size.

It was not all the fault of the public. They did not see the big Academy pictures as we see them now, but three-quarters finished. This was a standing complaint of critics and academicians alike. Constable's vacillating habit of mind became more marked in his last years. He could not settle on his subject till almost too late for the exhibition, to which it would go, as he said, " sadly deficient in paint." Even deaf, kindly old Stothard, the " painter's painter " of the day and Constable's friend, shook his head over the *Opening of Waterloo Bridge*—" Very unfinished, sir." The critics, of course, seized on this failing and hounded him savagely ; indeed, *Blackwood's* once had to print an apology under threat of legal action. " Constable's snow " they called the little white impastoed lights, which made the movement of the atmosphere. They hated his palette-knife technique as an offence to all connoisseurs of art—" conceited imbecility " —considering the sable brush the only decent instrument for an academician. The truth was that after the exhibition he was apt to work on a picture for one or two years, subtly and delicately glazing over the white impastoes —adapting a Dutch practice—and so softening the violence that had upset the critics.

Some of the bitterness, which the course of his life and his disappointments had bred in him, crept into his choice of landscape. Far away are the silvery water-meadows of the Salisbury days ; farther still the earlier simplicity of the Stour Valley scenes. Instead, there is a concentration on effects of storm, sometimes of tremendous power. " The Rainbow " (*Salisbury Cathedral from the Meadows*) is a *tour de force* of high drama. It was typical of him that he should have spent so much time throughout his life on the study of this " outstanding phenomenon " since, by tradition, it is symbolical of hope, and at the same time, it appears in the worst circumstances for the traveller. It remains, however, a colour problem of peculiar intensity, since the spectrum is uncompromising. It is worth comparing the little sketch of the *Double Rainbow* (Plate 46), of which the problem was the perspective of its beautiful arc, with the complications of the Salisbury scenes where the full play of brilliant colour compels exceedingly careful handling of the subsidiary tones.

It will have been seen that the careful drawing with the brush which marked the foregrounds of his picture up to 1820 has disappeared, and instead there is a freer impressionism. He discarded form and concentrated on mass, colour, and pattern. This was his offering to the impressionists of the nineteenth century, for his palette-knife technique contains seeds of the impressionist outlook and even of the doctrine of divisionism, which the pointillistes were to champion. The *Hampstead Heath* in the National Gallery of 1833 (Plate XII), *The Cenotaph* (Plate 149), and *Arundel Mill and Castle* (Plate 150) all show these qualities in their highest developments.

In another sense this period contains a new phase of Constable's art. No longer are his Academy pictures painted in the open air ; they are extremely conscientious studio works built up stage by stage from preliminary sketches. *The Opening of Waterloo Bridge* of 1832 in Lord Glenconner's collection was, for instance, a subject which he had studied for over fourteen years, constantly discarding variations of the scene which did not satisfy his standard (see Plates 127–132). For *The Valley Farm* of 1835 (Plate 142) we know at least three preliminary sketches apart from the large-scale working drawings for the trees in the Victoria and Albert Museum. He was, in fact, at last an older man ; no longer was he " weatherproof ", as his wife used to say, and capable of fatigue and exposure while sketching out of doors. Moreover, attacks of rheumatism made the labour of oil painting more onerous, and through these last years we find him working more than before in watercolour. For a complex of reasons—Ruskin's championship of Turner, a revolution of taste from the more dramatic in art which led to the rediscovery of the early English watercolour school, and perhaps to a certain doctrinaire purism—Constable's watercolours have never been popular. While Turner's fantastic dexterity in the medium has been praised and praised, Constable's ability has been stigmatized. It may perhaps be fair to say that he had not the tenderness for the medium that Turner had innately ; but his technique and the combinations in his later work of pen with watercolour, of scratchings-out glazed over, of blotted washes and the rest of the gamut entitle him to the highest rank as a technician. The spirit, too, controlling the technique is as lively, real, and sensitive as that which directs his oil paintings.

His art had been, to a remarkable degree, a progress of ideas successfully executed ; there is no stagnant period ; he does not lapse at middle age into repetition. As was fitting, his last period sums up the intention of his life, stating it by methods that are not so popular to-day because as pioneer work they compete with, and have been surpassed by, later adventurers in landscape. They do, however, summarize his attitude that light and movement makes the picture ; that the picture is independent of a subject—in his day an important discovery in æsthetics.

It was in this mood that he undertook the publication of a series of engravings in mezzotint from his pictures and sketches, known as the *English Landscape*. Begun in 1829, it was conceived partly as a statement of his views in a medium which would cause less criticism than his oils evoked, partly also as a counterblast of Turner's *Liber Studiorum*. David Lucas, whom Constable selected to work at his direction, produced in the most difficult circumstances a series of plates which, if seen in their best states before Constable had worn them out with endless and irritating alterations, surpass in some phases Turner's much-vaunted model. Turner relied primarily on etching for the strength of his design ; his original work as an etcher has, in many cases, obtained a special prominence for his plates, although the combination of etching and mezzotint is seldom happy after the first few dozen impressions have been run off. Constable, through Lucas, trusted pure mezzotint, preferring drypoint to reinforce small details of structure, and employing etching most rarely. It is a sad fate that, of the twenty-six plates which he finally published in four parts, almost all should have been ruined before they reached the printer by Constable's frequent changes of detail. After his death, Lucas published a second series, begun, in many cases, under Constable's direction, but unhampered by his zeal for something more than the plate would stand. In an odd way, these two publications, with Constable's death intervening, marked the shift of the generation. The first were printed on good paper under the direction of the man who was the last of the Old Masters and the first of the modern school ; and the second series came in an age on which the refinements of good paper were lost, and the massive though tough paper on which it was issued drank up half the ink that should have enriched their bloom.

If anyone wants to know the worst of Constable as a man, he can study the correspondence with Lucas ; observe the exasperating changes of plan, based though they were upon the highest motive of achieving the best result ; see the strange suspicion of his neighbour that rises unbidden in the breast of the best farmers ; watch waves of depression reduce him to an incapacity for decision, watch bitterness rouse an ungenerous pride that fettered Lucas to Constable, and jeopardized his whole career. When that has been said, the worst is over. Despite his faults Constable remains a lovable character. He was completely honest, and a hater of cant. It was his acute sense of humour that spilt over as vitriol in criticism—"caustic and merry," Derby Day Frith called him. And if he criticised, he was also generous in praise and generous in gratitude. The cabman who drove Leslie to the funeral has the last word : " I knew Mr. Constable, Sir ; and when I heard he was dead, I was as sorry as if he had been my own father—he was as nice a man as that, Sir."

Though he had his circle of friends among the artists, chiefly those like Wilkie, Leslie, Landseer, and their coterie who were revolting against the Italian tradition, he was the cat that walked by itself. Though he would speak freely of his performances—too freely, many of his contemporaries said—he had few pupils. John Dunthorne, the son of his first instructor, worked closely with him as his assistant, and his pictures have often been confounded with those of his master. Another man of great capacity, though an amateur, who knew Constable well and often sketched with him, was Thomas Churchyard of Woodbridge, Fitzgerald's friend, a man with as quick an eye for an effect of light as his tongue was quick for conversation or a bottle of port. John Chalon was one of the few recognized painters of the day who really felt the impress of his style in Constable's lifetime, though W. J. Muller was affected by him for a few years. Early work by F. R. Lee is also sometimes mistaken for Constable's and we know that, at the instance of his patron, William Wells of Redleaf, he even asked Constable to sell him some of his sketches—to which request the answer was very short.

Much of this essay has been devoted to Constable's large Academy pictures, because they were to him of the highest importance, as the fullest reasoned statements of his views on landscape, made for the public of the day. To-day, they are on the whole less prized than the smaller oil sketches, the first of *plein air* painting, which are much nearer to our own idiom. Many of them, however, are reproduced here. Æsthetically, they are the discovery of the last fifty years. At Constable's sale in 1838 they went in bundles for a few pounds a time. For some thirty years after his death little was heard of him. Then a further collection of his work came on the market after the death of his friend and biographer, Charles Leslie, and found a more receptive public, which had had, meanwhile, the chance to see some of the Constables bequeathed to the nation by Sheepshanks. In 1878 came the great exhibition of his work at the Grosvenor Gallery, derived principally from the resources of his children. But whereas the first force of his influence had been spent in France to be transmitted through Delacroix to the Impressionists, in England the second wave found, alas, only painters of secondary importance to absorb it, for instance, Leader, Wimperis, or Collier. Wilson Steer, Sickert and John found their way back to the main stream of the English tradition which Constable represents through the seed of it fertile still in Paris.

Besides the illustrations of Constable's work, a few plates have been chosen of painters such as Rubens and Ruysdael, from whom, as we have seen, Constable derived, and of his successors, for instance, Monet and Sisley. These single plates can do no more than suggest the ideas I have tried to elaborate in this introduction, though illustrations could be multiplied to emphasize its general thesis, that Constable focused the old tradition of landscape on to a point from which a new development could be made.

BIBLIOGRAPHY

Léon Bazalgette, *John Constable d'après les Souvenirs recueillis* par C. R. Leslie, 1905.
Lawrence Binyon, *English Watercolour*, 1933.
Burlington Magazine, 1904, 1913, 1916, 1935, 1937.
Catalogues of the Royal Academy Exhibitions, annotated by J. H. Anderdon.
Ernest Chesneau, *Peinture Anglaise*, 1882.
The Connoisseur, 1932, 1933, 1936, 1937.
Allan Cunningham, *Lives of the most eminent British Painters* (edited by Mrs. Heaton, 3 vols., 1880).
English Landscape Scenery, a Series of Forty Mezzotint Engravings on Steel by David Lucas from Pictures painted by John Constable, R.A., 1855.
Raymond Eschollier, *Delacroix, peintre, graveur, écrivain*, 3 vols., 1926–29.
André Fontainas, *Constable* (trans. W. Jackson), 1927.
Algernon Graves, *Exhibitors at the Royal Academy*, 8 vols., 1905–6.
—— *Exhibitors at the British Institution*, 1908.
—— *Century of Loan Exhibitions*, 5 vols., 1913–15.
James Greig (ed. by), *The Farington Diary*, 8 vols., 1922–28.
Sir C. J. Holmes, *Constable and his Influence on Landscape Painting*, 1902.
—— *Constable, Gainsborough, Lucas*, 1921.
André Joubin, *Journal de Delacroix*, 3 vols., 1932.
—— *Correspondance générale de Delacroix, 1804–1857*, 6 vols., 1936.
C. R. Leslie, *Memoirs of the Life of John Constable, R.A.*, 2nd edn., 1845.
—— *Memoirs of the Life of John Constable, R.A.*., edited and enlarged by the Hon. Andrew Shirley, 1937.
Peter Leslie, *Letters from John Constable, R.A., to C. R. Leslie, R.A.*, 1932.
E. V. Lucas, *John Constable, the Painter*, 1924.
The Earl of Plymouth, *John Constable, R.A.*, 1903.
Richard and Samuel Redgrave, *Century of British Painters*, 1st edn., 1866, 2nd edn., 1890.
Samuel Redgrave, *Dictionary of Painters of the English School*, 1874.
The Hon. Andrew Shirley, *The Published Mezzotints of David Lucas after John Constable, R.A.*, 1930.
—— *Bonington*, 1940.
—— *see also* C. R. Leslie, *supra*.
W. T. Witley, *Art in England, 1800–1820*, 1929.
—— *Art in England, 1821–1837*, 1930.

CHRONOLOGY

of the principal events in Constable's life and of his exhibited pictures
(Abbreviations: R.A., Royal Academy; B.I., British Institution)

1776 Born at East Bergholt, Suffolk, 11th June.
1795 First journey to London.
1797 Abandons painting to work for his father.
1798 Second journey to London: introduced to Farington.
1799 Established in London; copies Wilson.
1800 Admitted student at the R.A. Visits Suffolk.
1801 Studies in London. Visits Suffolk; Derbyshire.
1802 R.A. *Landscape.* Visits Suffolk.
1803 R.A. Two *Landscapes*; two *Studies from Nature.*
Voyage by sea, London to Deal.
1804 Works in London. Visits Suffolk.
1805 R.A. *Landscape, moonlight.* Visits Kent.
1806 R.A. watercolour, *H.M.S. Victory in the Battle of Trafalgar.*
Visits the Lakes; Suffolk; Surrey.
1807 R.A. *View in Westmorland; Keswick Lake; Bow Fell, Cumberland.*
Visits Epsom; copies portraits at Ham House.
1808 R.A. *Scene in Cumberland; Windermere Lake.* B.I. *Scene in Westmorland; Moonlight.*
Visits Suffolk.
1809 R.A. Three *Landscapes.* B.I. *Borrowdale; A Cottage; Keswick Lake; Windermere Lake.*
Visits Malvern Hall, Warwickshire.
1810 R.A. *Landscape; A Churchyard.*
1811 R.A. *Twilight, Dedham Vale.* B.I. *A Church Porch.*
Engagement to Maria Bicknell.
Visits Salisbury; Stourhead; Suffolk; Worcester.
1812 R.A. *A Watermill; View of Salisbury; Landscape, recent shower; Autumnal Sunset.*
Visits Suffolk.
1813 R.A. *Landscape, boys fishing; Landscape, morning.* B.I. *Scene in Suffolk.*
Unsuccessful candidate for A.R.A.
Visits Staffordshire.
1814 R.A. *A Plowing Scene in Suffolk; A Ferry.* B.I. *Marten Cats; View on the Stour.*
Visits Suffolk; South Essex.
1815 R.A. *Boatbuilding, Flatford; View of Dedham; A Village in Suffolk; Landscape; A Sketch;* three drawings. B.I. *Landscape.*
Death of Constable's mother.
Visits Suffolk.
1816 R.A. *A Wheatfield; A Wood, autumn.*
Death of Constable's father.
Marriage to Maria Bicknell.
Unsuccessful candidate for A.R.A.
Visits Norfolk; Suffolk; Dorset.

CHRONOLOGY

1817 R.A. *Wivenhoe Park ; A Cottage ; The Rev. John Fisher ; Scene on a Navigable River (Flatford Mill).* B.I. *Harvest Field with Reapers and Gleaners.*
Unsuccessful candidate for A.R.A.
Birth of John Charles Constable, 1817–1841.
Visits Suffolk.

1818 R.A. *Landscape, breaking up of a shower ;* (drawings) *Gothic Porch ; Group of Elms.* B.I. *Cottage in a Cornfield ; Scene on the banks of a River.*
Unsuccessful candidate for A.R.A.
Visits Suffolk.

1819 R.A. *A Scene on the River Stour* (*The White Horse*) bought by Fisher.
Elected A.R.A.
Birth of Maria Louisa Constable, 1819–1884.
Visits East Bergholt.

1820 R.A. *Stratford Mill,* bought by Tinney ; *View of Harwich Lighthouse.*
Visits Salisbury ; Dorset ; New Forset ; Warwickshire (Malvern Hall).

1821 R.A. *The Haywain ; Hampstead Heath ; A Shower ; Harrow.*
Unsuccessful candidate for R.A.
Birth of Charles Golding Constable, 1821–1879.
Visits Berkshire ; Oxford ; Salisbury.

1822 R.A. *View on the Stour ; Hampstead Heath ; Malvern Hall, View of the Terrace ; Hampstead ; A Study of Trees from Nature.*
Arrowsmith negotiates for purchase of *The Haywain.*
Unsuccessful candidate for R.A.
Visits Brighton.

1823 R.A. *Salisbury Cathedral from the Bishop's Garden ; A Study of Trees, a sketch ; A Cottage ; Yarmouth Jetty.* B.I. *Stratford Mill.*
Birth of Isabel Constable, 1823–1885.
Visits Dorset ; Cole Orton, Leicestershire.

1824 R.A. *The Lock,* bought by Morrison.
Paris. *The Haywain, Hampstead Heath, Lock on the Stour.*
Arrowsmith buys *The Haywain* and two others ; commissions seven more. Schroth commissions three.
Visits Brighton.

1825 R.A. *The Leaping Horse ; Hampstead Heath, Windsor in distance ; Hampstead Heath, Harrow in distance.* B.I. *The White Horse ; Stratford Mill.*
Lille, *The White Horse.*
Receives commissions from Paris for eight pictures.
Awarded Gold Medal for his pictures at the Salon.
Birth of Emily Constable, 1825–1839.
Visits Brighton.

1826 R.A. *The Cornfield,* bought for the nation, 1838 ; *A Mill, Gillingham ; A Dell, Helmingham,* bought by Pulham.
Awarded gold medal at the Lille Exhibition.
Birth of Alfred Constable, 1826–1853.
Visits Brighton.

1827 R.A. *The Chain Pier, Brighton ; Watermill, Gillingham.* B.I. *The Cornfield, The Glebe Farm ; Gillingham Mill.*
Moves to Well Walk, Hampstead.

Visits Suffolk ; Brighton.
1828 R.A. *Dedham Vale ; Hampstead Heath.* B.I. *The Chain Pier, Brighton.*
Birth of Lionel Bicknell Constable, 1828–1884.
Unsuccessful candidate for R.A.
Illness and death of Mrs. Constable.
Visits Brighton.
1829 R.A. *Hadleigh Castle ; Landscape.* B.I. *Landscape and Lock ; Landscape, Cottage Scene.*
Elected R.A.
Begins work on the *English Landscape* with David Lucas.
Visits Salisbury.
1830 R.A. *Dell in Helmingham Park ; View of Hampstead Heath ; Landscape.*
On the Hanging Committee of the R.A. and visitor of the Life Class.
Issues first two parts of the *English Landscape.*
1831 *Salisbury Cathedral from the Meadows* (*The Rainbow*).
Issues third and fourth parts of the *English Landscape.*
Visits Suffolk.
1832 R.A. *The Opening of Waterloo Bridge ; Sir Richard Steele's Cottage ; Hampstead ; A Romantic House, Hampstead ;* drawings : *Jaques and the Wounded Stag ; A Church ; A Mill ; Farm House.*
Issues fifth and last part of the *English Landscape.*
Visits Suffolk.
1833 R.A. *Englefield House ; A Heath, showery noon ; A Cottage in a Cornfield ; Landscape Sunset ;* watercolours : *An Old Farmhouse ; A Miller's House ; A Windmill, squally day.*
Visits Suffolk.
1834 R.A. Watercolours : *Old Sarum ; Stoke Poges Church ; Interior of a Church ;* drawing : *Study of Trees, Hampstead.*
B.I. *A Cottage in a Cornfield ; A Heath ; Dedham Vale.*
Birmingham. *The Rainbow.*
Worcester. *Barge on the Stour.*
Visits Sussex.
1835 R.A. *The Valley Farm,* bought by Vernon.
Worcester. *The Cornfield ; Dedham Vale ; Flatford Mill.*
Lectures on landscape at Hampstead, and Worcester.
Visits Sussex ; Worcester.
1836 R.A. *The Cenotaph ;* watercolour, *Stonehenge.*
Four lectures on landscape at the Royal Institution.
1837 R.A. *Arundel Mill and Castle.*
Visitor at the Life Class.
Death, 1st April.

LIST OF ILLUSTRATIONS

In Colour

In Monochrome

LIST OF ILLUSTRATIONS

LIST OF ILLUSTRATIONS

PLATES

MRS. CONSTABLE
(Colchester, The Albert Hall and Art Gallery)

GOLDING CONSTABLE
(By permission of the Ipswich Art Gallery)

JOHN CONSTABLE AT THE LIFE CLASS,
by Daniel Maclise
(London. The National Portrait Gallery)

JOHN CONSTABLE, *by R. R. Reinagle*
(London. The National Portrait Gallery)

MRS. MARIA CONSTABLE
(*London. The National Gallery, 2655*)

MRS. MARIA CONSTABLE
(*Collection of D. H. Leggatt, Esq.*)

DEDHAM VALE, SUFFOLK
(London. The Victoria and Albert Museum, 124)

THE ANNUNCIATION, *by Claude*
(London. The National Gallery, 61)

LANDSCAPE, EVENING
(*London. The Victoria and Albert Museum*, 587)

Photo: A. C. Cooper

SUMMIT OF CADER IDRIS, *by R. Wilson*
(*London. The National Gallery*, 5596)

VALLEY SCENE WITH TREES

(London. The Victoria and Albert Museum, 142)

TREES BY A POND, *by T. Gainsborough*

VALLEY SCENE

(Collection of P. M. Turner, Esq.)

THE BANKS OF A RIVER, *by J. Van Ruysdael*

(Edinburgh. The National Gallery)

SUNSET

(*London. The Victoria and Albert Museum*, 585)

CHATEAU DE STEEN, *by P. P. Rubens*

(*London. The National Gallery*, 157)

ON THE STOUR
(*London. The Diploma Gallery, Burlington House*)

TREES IN FONTAINBLEAU FOREST, *by Théodore Rousseau*
(*London. Victoria and Albert Museum, C.A.I.,* 54)

DEDHAM WATER MILL *Photo: Knoedler*

(*London. Collection of R. H. Bathurst, Esq.*)

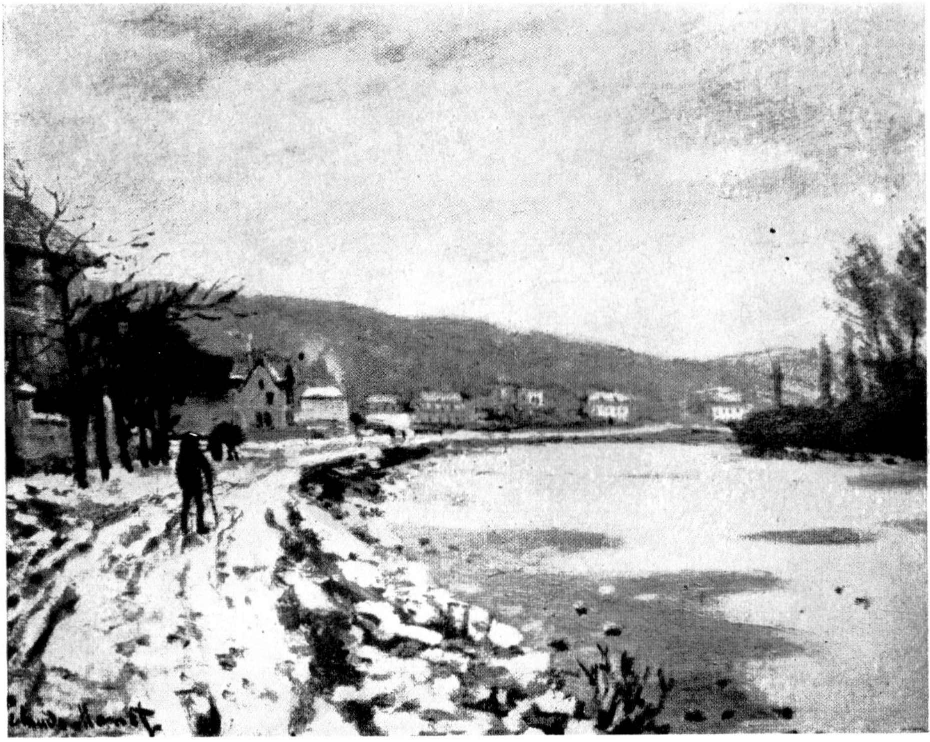

LA SEINE A ROUEN, *by C. Monet*

THE WHITE HORSE
(*New York. J. Pierpont Morgan Library*)

APRES-MIDI DE MAI, *by A. Sisley*

DR. GRIMWOOD

(*Colchester. The Albert Hall and Art Gallery*)

ARCHDEACON JOHN FISHER

(*With the Trustees of the late Rev. O. P. Fisher*)

WILLIAM WATTS RUSSELL
(Courtesy of Messrs. Knoedler & Co.)

DR. WINGFIELD
(Collection of Professor W. G. Constable, M.A., F.S.A.)

MR. HOBSON OF MARKFIELD AND FAMILY
(*Collection of L. G. Duke, Esq.*)

THE BRIDGES FAMILY
(*Collection of Captain J. W. Bridges*)

WILLIAM FISHER

(With the Trustees of the late Rev. O. P. Fisher)

HEAD OF A GIRL

(London. Victoria and Albert Museum, 1255)

MISS MARIA CONSTABLE AS A CHILD
(Collection of the late Willoughby S. Smith, Esq.)

MOTHER AND CHILD
(Collection of P. M. Turner, Esq.)

JOHN CONSTABLE, *by his son, Charles Constable*
(Collection of the late Willoughby S. Smith, Esq.)

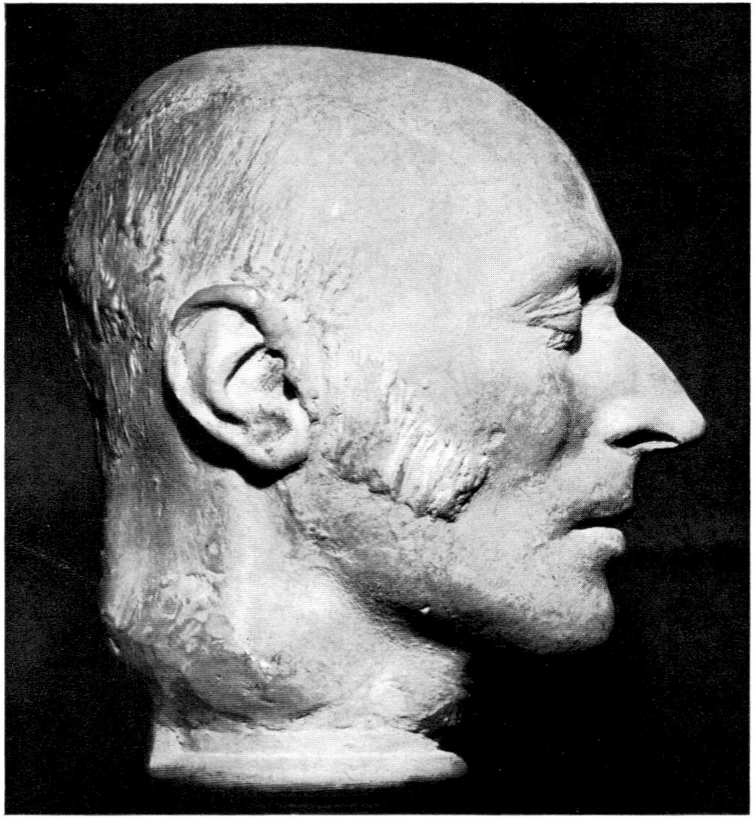

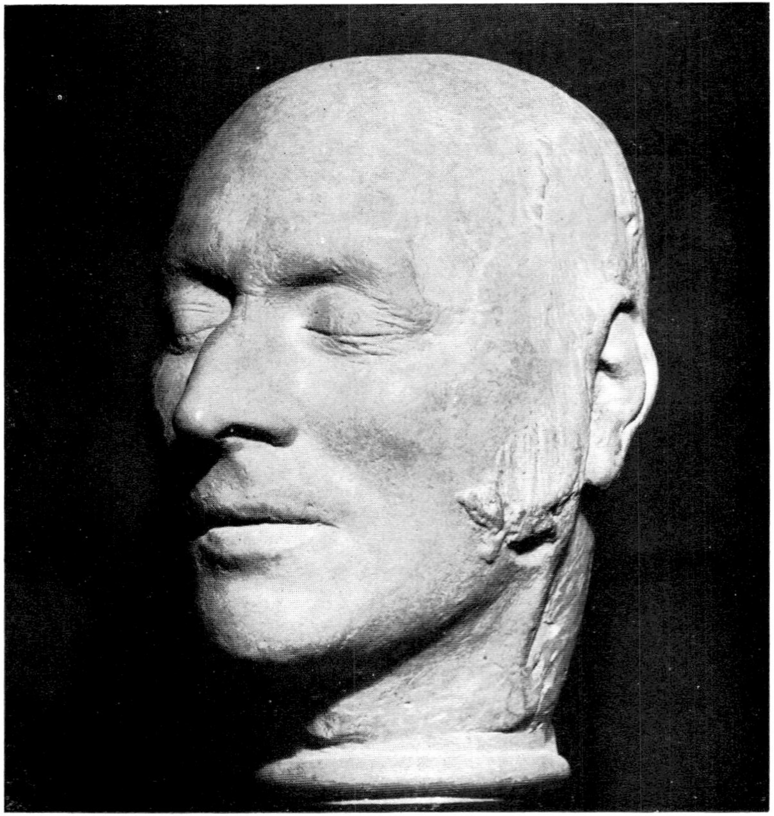

DEATH MASK OF JOHN CONSTABLE, *by E. Davis*
(Collection of H. G. Constable, Esq.)

LANGFORD CHURCH

(Collection of the late Sir Michael Sadler, K.C.S.I., C.B.)

Plate 20

BROOK, TREES AND MEADOWS

(Collection of the late Sir Michael Sadler, K.C.S.I., C.B.)

WINDSOR
(*London. Victoria and Albert Museum*, 804-1888)

MAM TOR
(*London. Victoria and Albert Museum*, 247e–1888)

CHATSWORTH (*Collection of P. M. Turner, Esq.*)

LAMARSH HOUSE (*Courtesy of Messrs. Vicars Bros.*)

STOUR VALLEY (*Collection of P. M. Turner, Esq.*)

WINDMILL (*London. Victoria and Albert Museum*, 841–1888)

EDGE OF A WOOD

(Courtesy of Messrs. Gooden & Fox)

BRANTHAM ALTARPIECE

(Brantham Church)

BARNES COMMON

(*London. The Tate Gallery* 1066)

THE WATERMILL, *by Meindert Hobbema*

(*Dresden. Royal Gallery*)

TREES AND MEADOWS

(Collection of the late Sir Michael Sadler, K.C.S.I., C.B.)

Plate 28

TREES, HELMINGHAM

(*London. The Victoria and Albert Museum* 598)

VIEW IN KENT

(Collection of P. M. Turner, Esq.)

Plate 30

HELVELLYN
(Collection of P. M. Turner, Esq.)

LANGDALE

(Collection of P. M. Turner, Esq.)

VIEW IN THE LAKES

(London. Victoria and Albert Museum, 1257–1888)

KESWICK LAKE

(Collection of the late Sir Michael Sadler, K.C.S.I., C.B.)

STOKE BY NAYLAND (*London. The National Gallery*, 2649)

EPSOM (*London. The Tate Gallery*, 1818)

NAYLAND ALTARPIECE

(*Nayland Church*)

STOURHEAD, WILTS:
THE GARDENS OF SIR RICHARD COLT HOARE
(Collection of Sir Robert Witt, C.B.E., F.S.A.)

MILFORD BRIDGE
(London. British Museum)

EAST BERGHOLT CHURCH PORCH

(*London. The National Gallery*, 1245)

HOUSE AMONG TREES AND CORNFIELD

(Formerly collection of P. M. Turner, Esq.)

SHIPPING ON THE ORWELL *(London. Victoria and Albert Museum, 160)*

VIEW AT DEDHAM (*London. Victoria and Albert Museum,* 134–1888)

CART ON A COUNTRY ROAD (*London. Victoria and Albert Museum,* 326–1888)

BARGES ON THE STOUR
(*London Victoria and Albert Museum, 325*)

Photo: A. C. Cooper

DEDHAM VALE

(Collection of the late Granville Proby, Esq.)

LOCKS AND COTTAGES ON THE STOUR
(*London. Victoria and Albert Museum*, 135–1888)

VILLAGE FAIR

(*London. The Victoria and Albert Museum, 128*)

MILL STREAM
(*London. The National Gallery*, 1816)

AUTUMNAL SUNSET
(London. Victoria and Albert Museum, 127–1888)

VALLEY OF THE STOUR
(Collection of T. W. Bacon, Esq.)

Photo: A. C. Cooper

HAYFIELD, SUNSET
(*London. Victoria and Albert Museum*, 121–1888)

UPLAND PARK
(*London. Victoria and Albert Museum*, 146–1888)

LANDSCAPE WITH DOUBLE RAINBOW
(*London. Victoria and Albert Museum*, 328–1888)

HAMPSTEAD HEATH

(Collection of the late Sir Michael Sadler, K.C.S.I., C.B.)

THE LOCK ON THE STOUR

(From the Hartree Family Collection)

SPRING : EAST BERGHOLT COMMON
(*London, Victoria and Albert Museum, No.* 144–1888)

CART AND HORSES
(*London. Victoria and Albert Museum*, 333–1888)

FLOWER STUDY

(London, Victoria and Albert Museum, 581–1888)

FLOWER STUDY

(London. Victoria and Albert Museum, 582–1888)

VALE OF DEDHAM
(Leeds. Corporation Art Gallery)

Plate 52

GOLDING CONSTABLE'S GARDEN
(*London. Victoria and Albert Museum, 623-1888*)

BOATBUILDING, FLATFORD

(London. Victoria and Albert Museum, 37)

SUMMER MORNING

(*Courtesy of Messrs. Vicars Bros.*)

Photo: A. C. Cooper

SUMMER MORNING

(*London. Victoria and Albert Museum*, 132–1888)

STUDY OF AN ELM TREE
(*London. Victoria and Albert Museum*, 786–1888)

CORNFIELD WITH FIGURES

(*London. The National Gallery, 1065*)

SOUTHEND *(London. Victoria and Albert Museum,* D228–1888)

FEERING CHURCH, KELVEDON, ESSEX *(Manchester. Whitworth Art Gallery)*

WEYMOUTH BAY

(*London. The National Gallery*, 2652)

COTTAGE IN A CORNFIELD

(*London. Victoria and Albert Museum*, 1631–1888)

SKETCH FOR DEDHAM MILL AND CHURCH
(*London. Victoria and Albert Museum*, 145–1888)

SKETCH FOR DEDHAM MILL AND CHURCH
(*London. The National Art Gallery*, 2661)

STRATFORD MILL

(*London. Walter Hutchinson, Esq.*)

DISTANT VIEW OF SALISBURY
(Collection of P. M. Turner, Esq.)

SALISBURY

(London. The National Gallery, 2651)

THE CLOSE, SALISBURY

(Cambridge. Fitzwilliam Museum)

FLATFORD MILL
(*London, National Gallery, No.* 1273)

Plate IV

VIEW NEAR SALISBURY

(London. Victoria and Albert Museum, No. 153–1888)

THE CLOSE, SALISBURY
(London. Victoria and Albert Museum, 318)

Plate 66

SKETCH FOR THE HAYWAIN (*Actual size of painting*) (*Collection of Mrs. L. W. Vicars*)

SKETCH FOR THE HAYWAIN

(London. Victoria and Albert Museum, 987)

MALVERN HALL

(Collection of Marsden J. Perry, Esq., Providence, Rhode Island, U.S.A.)

MALVERN HALL

(Musée du Mans)

Plate 70

MALVERN HALL

(London. The National Gallery, 2653)

THE SALT BOX

(*London. The National Gallery*, 1236)

PERNES MILL, GILLINGHAM (*Cambridge. Fitzwilliam Museum*)

VALLEY NEAR SALISBURY (*Collection of T. W. Bacon, Esq.*)

KNOWLE HALL, WARWICKSHIRE (*London. Victoria and Albert Museum*, 617–1888)

COTTAGES, NEW FOREST (*London. Victoria and Albert Museum*, 297–1888)

WATERMILL, NEWBURY (*London. Victoria and Albert Museum*, 285–1888)

ABINGDON FROM THE RIVER (*London. Victoria and Albert Museum*, 618–1888)

TREES NEAR HAMPSTEAD

(*London, Victoria and Albert Museum*, 1630–1888)

VIEW ON THE STOUR

(Courtesy of the Henry E. Huntington Library and Art Gallery, California, U.S.A.)

SKETCH FOR VIEW ON THE STOUR

(Courtesy of Mrs. L. W. Vicars)

MEZZOTINT, *by David Lucas, of* VIEW ON THE STOUR
(London. British Museum)

SKETCH FOR VIEW ON THE STOUR
(By permission of the Trustees of the Royal Holloway College)

YARMOUTH PIER

(Collection of Lord Glenconner)

CORNFIELDS AT BRIGHTON

(Collection of Sir Felix Cassel, Bart.)

LANDSCAPE WITH TREES AND FIGURES

(London. Victoria and Albert Museum, 165–1888)

STRATFORD ST. MARY

(Formerly collection of P. M. Turner, Esq.)

THE HAY-WAIN
(*London. National Gallery, No.* 1207)

SALISBURY CATHEDRAL

(*London. Victoria and Albert Museum No.* 33)

SKETCH FOR SALISBURY CATHEDRAL FROM THE BISHOP'S GARDEN

(Collection of T. W. Bacon, Esq.)

SALISBURY CATHEDRAL FROM THE BISHOP'S GARDEN

(New York. U.S.A. The Frick Collection)

HELMINGHAM DELL
(Collection of T. W. Bacon, Esq.)

GILLINGHAM BRIDGE
(London. The National Gallery, 1244)

GILLINGHAM BRIDGE
(With the Trustees of the late Rev. O. P. Fisher)

HAMPSTEAD HEATH
(*London. The National Gallery*, 1813)

TREES AT STAUNTON HAROLD

(London. Victoria and Albert Museum, 356–1888)

BOY RIDING THROUGH A WOOD

(Formerly collection of P. M. Turner, Esq.)

WILLY LOTT'S HOUSE, NEAR FLATFORD (*Collection of P. M. Turner, Esq.*)

THE LOCK

(Collection of S. Morrison, Esq.)

SKETCH FOR THE LOCK
(Collection of P. M. Turner, Esq.)

COAST SCENE WITH FISHING BOATS

(London. Victoria and Albert Museum, 129–1888)

BRIGHTON BEACH *(London. Victoria and Albert Museum,* 782–1888)

SEA BEACH, BRIGHTON

(Collection of the late Willoughby S. Smith, Esq.)

WINDMILL AND RAINBOW

(London. Victoria and Albert Museum, 126–1888)

FIRST STUDY FOR THE LEAPING HORSE
(*London. British Museum*, 10a)

STUDY FOR THE LEAPING HORSE
(*Collection of H. Blaiberg, Esq.*)

SKETCH FOR THE LEAPING HORSE

(London. Victoria and Albert Museum, 986)

HAMPSTEAD HEATH

(*Formerly in the collection of Sir Joseph Beecham, Bart.*)

Photo: Sir Robert Witt Collection

HAMPSTEAD HEATH

(*Formerly in the collection of Sir Joseph Beecham, Bart.*)

Photo: Sir Robert Witt Collection

MORNING CLOUDS (*Collection of the late Sir Michael Sadler, K.C.S.I., C.B.*)

CLOUD STUDY (*London. The Victoria and Albert Museum, 168–1888*)

WINDMILL AND SHEEP

(*London. Victoria and Albert Museum, No.* 173–1888)

THE LEAPING HORSE

(London. Diploma Gallery, Burlington House)

CLOUD STUDY
(*London. Victoria and Albert Museum*, 7841)

CLOUD STUDY
(*Collection of T. W. Bacon, Esq.*)

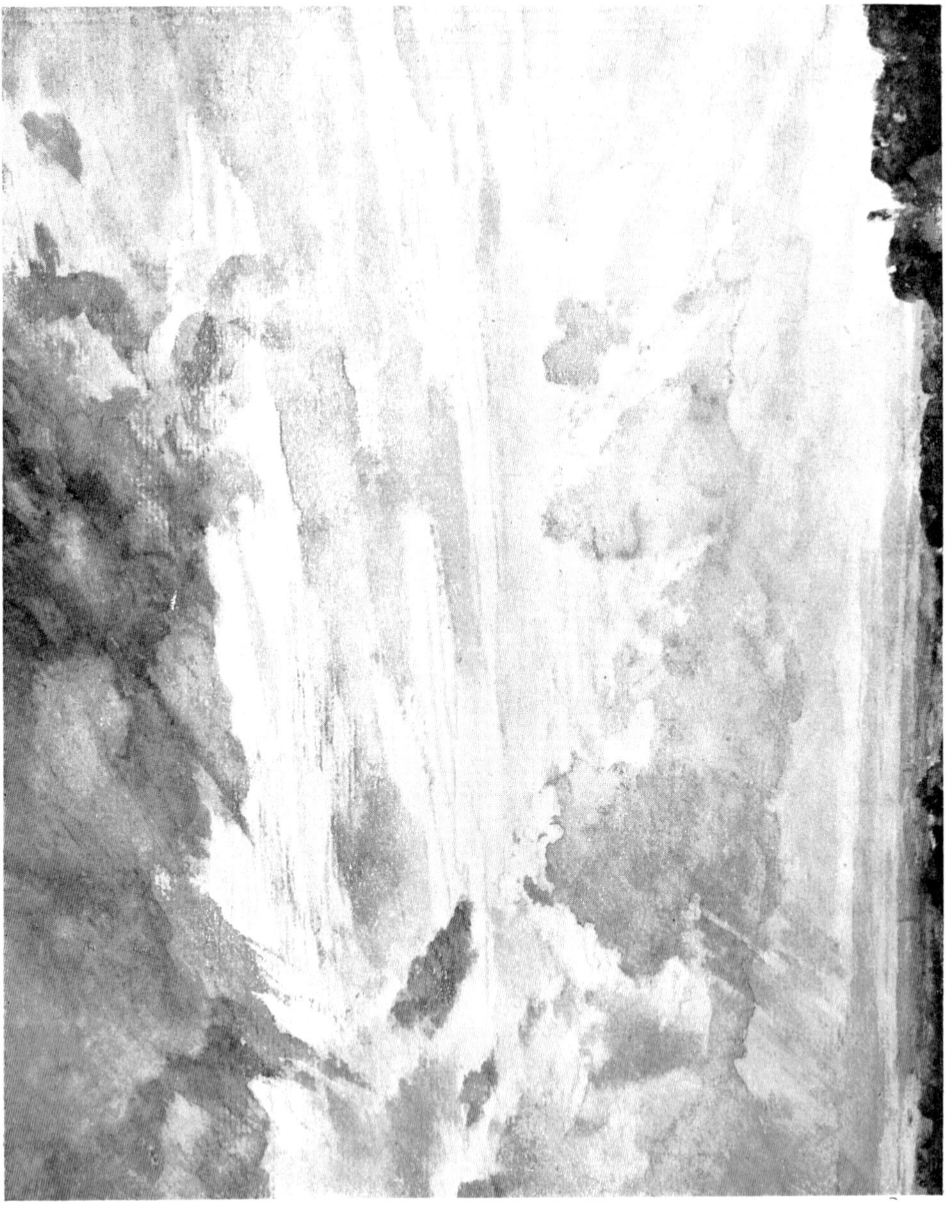

CLOUD STUDY

(*London. Victoria and Albert Museum, 240*)

STUDY FOR THE CORNFIELD
(Collection of T. W. Bacon, Esq.)

EDGE OF A WOOD
(Courtesy of Messrs. Leggatt Bros.)

A COUNTRY LANE

(*London. The National Gallery*, 1821)

HELMINGHAM DELL
(*Collection of P. M. Turner, Esq.*)

THE GLEBE FARM

(*London. The National Gallery*, 1274)

STUDY OF HOUSE AND TREES

(*London. Victoria and Albert Museum*, 161)

SKETCH FOR THE GLEBE FARM

(*London. The Tate Gallery*, 1823)

HAMPSTEAD HEATH LOOKING TOWARDS HARROW

(Manchester. City Art Gallery)

GILLINGHAM MILL

(*London. Victoria and Albert Museum*, 1632–1888)

MARINE PARADE AND CHAIN PIER, BRIGHTON

(Collection of Lt.-Col. A. C. Sheepshanks)

COAST SCENE, STORMY WEATHER
(*London. Diploma Gallery, Burlington House*)

OLD SARUM, WILTSHIRE (*London. Victoria and Albert Museum*, 163–1888)

SUMMER AFTERNOON (*London. The National Gallery*, 1815)

SUMMER AFTERNOON AFTER A SHOWER

(Collection of P. M. Turner, Esq.)

MRS. CONSTABLE ASLEEP

(Collection of the late Willoughby S. Smith, Esq.)

HADLEIGH CASTLE

(*London. The National Gallery*, 4810)

SKETCH FOR HADLEIGH CASTLE

(Collection of T. W. Bacon, Esq.)

THE CORNFIELD
(*London. National Gallery, No.* 130)

Plate X

DEDHAM VALE

(Edinburgh. National Gallery)

WATER-MEADOWS NEAR SALISBURY

(Oxford Ashmolean Museum)

HAMPSTEAD HEATH

(Collection of Lord Ivor Spencer Churchill)

JACQUES AND THE WOUNDED STAG

(London. British Museum)

STUDY OF TREE STEMS

(*London. Victoria and Albert Museum*, 323–1888)

DELL, HELMINGHAM

(*London. The Tate Gallery*, 2660)

COUNTRY ROAD WITH FIGURES
(*London. Victoria and Albert Museum, 787*)

STUDY OF NUDE BASED ON A FIGURE IN THE LAST JUDGEMENT
(Collection of H. G. Constable, Esq.)

LIFE STUDY
(Collection of H. G. Constable, Esq.)

TREES AND WATER ON THE STOUR
(*London, Victoria and Albert Museum*, 250–1888)

DEDHAM CHURCH
(*London. Victoria and Albert Museum*, 249–1888)

MEZZOTINT, *by David Lucas, of* SALISBURY CATHEDRAL FROM THE MEADOWS

(*London. Victoria and Albert Museum*, 1250–1888)

SKETCH FOR SALISBURY CATHEDRAL FROM THE MEADOWS

(*London. The National Gallery*, 1814)

DRAWING CONNECTED WITH SALISBURY CATHEDRAL FROM THE MEADOWS
(Collection of L. G. Duke, Esq.)

Plate 122

CORONATION PROCESSION OF WILLIAM IV

(Formerly collection of P. M. Turner, Esq.)

CROSSING THE FORD

(London. The Guildhall)

STOKE-BY-NAYLAND (*London. Victoria and Albert Museum*, 150–1888)

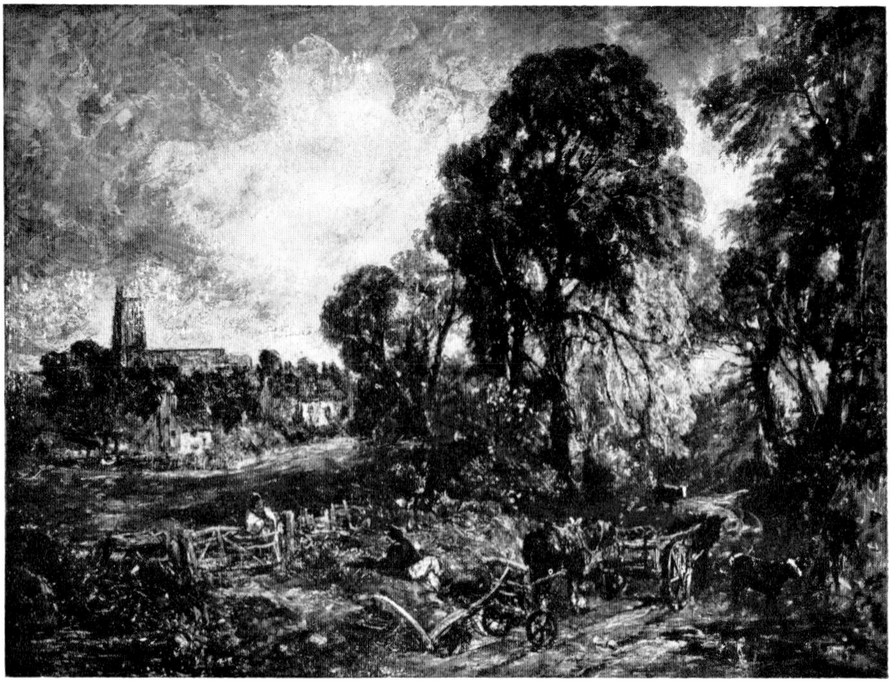

VIEW AT STOKE-BY-NAYLAND *Photo: Messrs. M. Knoedler & Co.*

THE WATER-MEADOWS NEAR SALISBURY

(London. Victoria and Albert Museum, 38)

ROMANTIC HOUSE, HAMPSTEAD
(London. The National Gallery, 1246)

ROMANTIC HOUSE, HAMPSTEAD
(Berlin, National Gallery)

OPENING OF WATERLOO BRIDGE
(London. Victoria and Albert Museum, 290)

SKETCH FOR THE OPENING OF WATERLOO BRIDGE
(London. The Diploma Gallery, Burlington House)

SKETCH FOR THE OPENING OF WATERLOO BRIDGE
(Formerly The Redfern Gallery)

HAMPSTEAD HEATH
(*London. National Gallery, No.* 1275)

Plate XII

STUDY OF POPPIES

(*London. Victoria and Albert Museum, No.* 329'88)

OPENING OF WATERLOO BRIDGE
(Collection of Lord Camrose)

SKETCH FOR THE OPENING OF WATERLOO BRIDGE

(*London. Victoria and Albert Museum*, 604–1888)

SKETCH FOR THE OPENING OF WATERLOO BRIDGE

(*London. Victoria and Albert Museum*, 322–1888)

OPENING OF WATERLOO BRIDGE

(Collection of Lord Fairhaven)

OPENING OF WATERLOO BRIDGE (WHITEHALL STAIRS)

(Collection of Lord Glenconner)

RUSTIC COTTAGES AT EAST BERGHOLT

(*London. Victoria and Albert Museum*, 229–1888)

COTTAGES AT EAST BERGHOLT

(*London. Victoria and Albert Museum*, 232–1888)

HAMPSTEAD
(London. British Museum)

RIVER AND BARGES
(London. Victoria and Albert Museum, 237–1888)

VIEW OVER LONDON FROM HAMPSTEAD

(London. Victoria and Albert Museum, 220)

HILLY COUNTRY

(London. Victoria and Albert Museum, 176–1888)

MEZZOTINT *by David Lucas, of* STONEHENGE
(*Collection of Victor Rienaeker, Esq.*)

MEZZOTINT, *by David Lucas, of* SUMMERLAND
(*London. British Museum*)

HAMPSTEAD HEATH (*Collection of Sir Alfred Harmsworth, Bart.*) *Photo: A. C. Cooper*

A SLUICE ON THE STOUR
(*London. Victoria and Albert Museum*, 131–1888)

AVENUE AT HAM HOUSE

(*London. Victoria and Albert Museum*, 818–1888)

FITTLEWORTH MILL

(*London. Victoria and Albert Museum*, 215–1888)

A RUSTIC BUILDING

(*London. Victoria and Albert Museum*, 133–1888)

LANDSCAPE STUDY, NEAR FLATFORD MILL

(*London. Victoria and Albert Museum*, 141–1888)

THE VALLEY FARM

(*London. The National Gallery*, 327)

SKETCH FOR THE VALLEY FARM

(London. Victoria and Albert Museum, 143–1888)

STUDY FOR THE VALLEY FARM
(*London. Victoria and Albert Museum*, 1249-1888)

STUDY FOR THE VALLEY FARM
(*London. Victoria and Albert Museum*, 1248-1888)

COUNTRY ROAD AND SANDBANK
(London. Victoria and Albert Museum, 327)

STONEHENGE
(*London. Victoria and Albert Museum, 1629*)

STUDIES FOR STONEHENGE

(147. *London. Victoria and Albert Museum*)

(147a. *London. British Museum*) (147b. *London. Victoria and Albert Museum*)

WORCESTER FROM THE NORTH
(*London. Victoria and Albert Museum*, 314–1888)

COTTAGE AND WATERMILL
(*London. Victoria and Albert Museum*, 208–1888)

THE CENOTAPH
(*London. The National Gallery,* 1272)

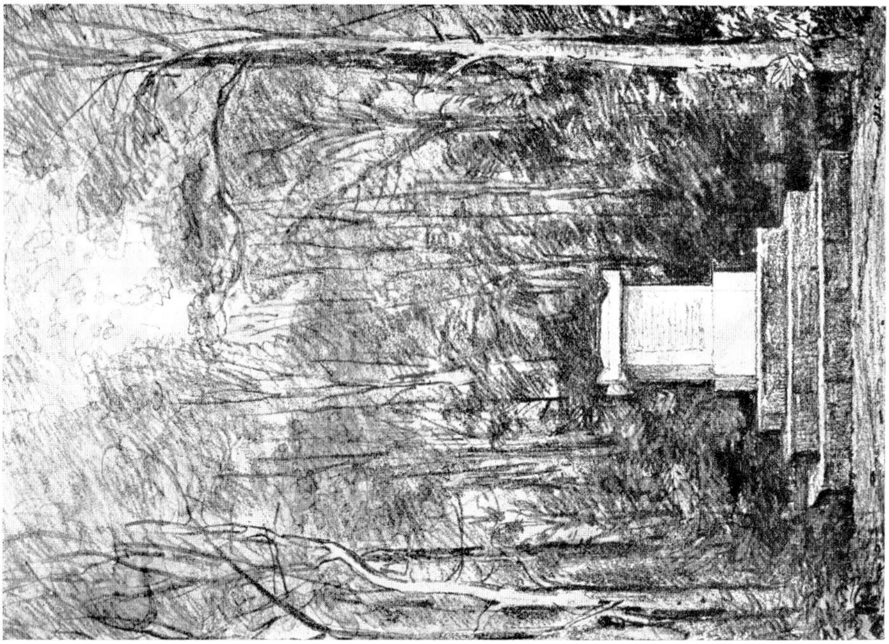

DRAWING FOR THE CENOTAPH
(*London. Victoria and Albert Museum,* 835–1888)

ARUNDEL MILL AND CASTLE

(Collection of Edward Drummond Libbey, Esq., Toledo, U.S.A.)

COBDEN'S ELECTION

(Collection of the late Willoughby S. Smith, Esq.)

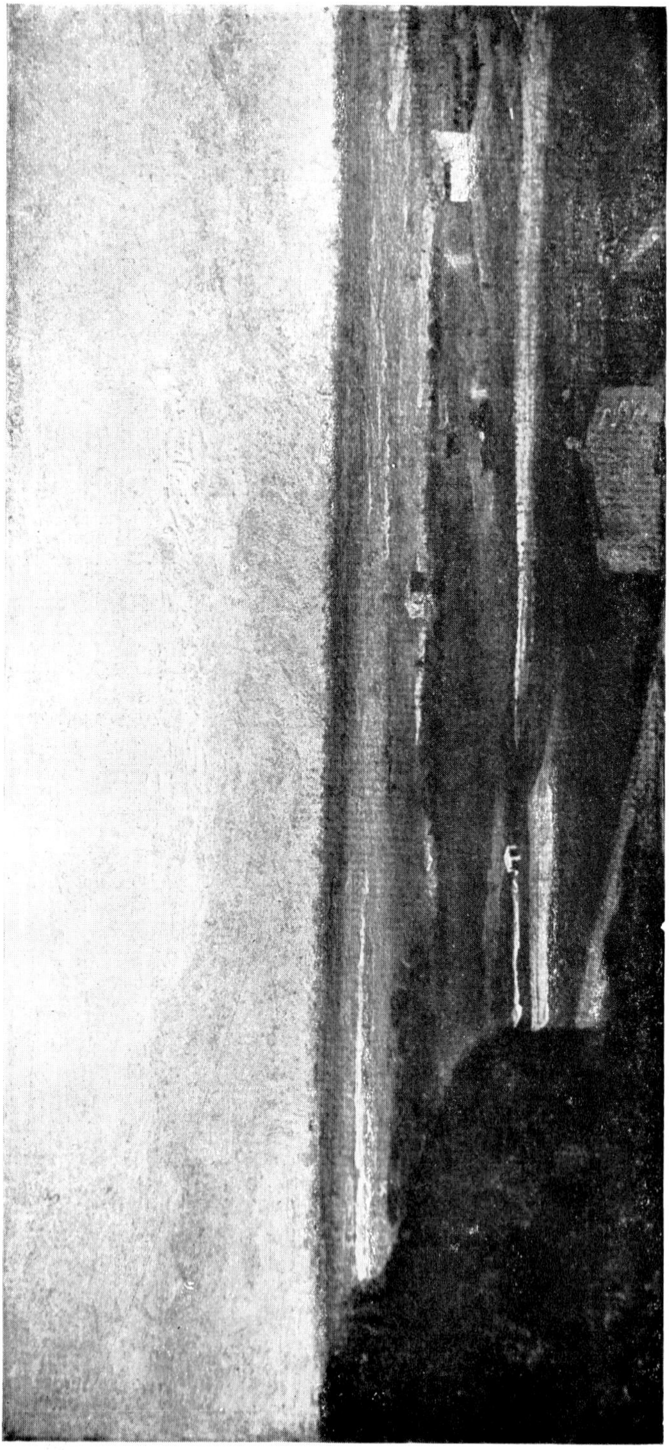

DISTANT VIEW OF MOUNTAINS

(Collection of the late Sir Hickman Bacon, Bart.)

NEAR FLATFORD

(Winchester Charles Bostock Esq.)

LANDSCAPE COMPOSITION

(Formerly collection of P. M. Turner, Esq.)

Plate 154

HILLY LANDSCAPE
(*Oxford. Ashmolean Museum*)

GIRL WEARING A SCARF
(Collection of the late Sir Hickman Bacon, Bart.)

PORTRAIT OF A MAN (? Bishop Fisher)
(Exeter. Collection of the late Robert Worthington, Esq., F.R.C.S.)

HOUSE AND GARDEN, HAMPSTEAD

(Collection of P. M. Turner, Esq.)

VIEW OF GREENWICH

(Formerly collection of P. M. Turner, Esq.)

LANDSCAPE

(Collection of P. M. Turner, Esq.)

RAINBOW (HAMPSTEAD HEATH)

(London. Lockett Thomson, Esq.)

DEVIL'S DYKE, BRIGHTON
(London. Collection of P, M. Turner, Esq.)

PORTRAIT OF A GIRL

(*London. H. A. Sutch, Esq.*)